I0137926

25 SIMPLE TRUTHS ON *Marriage*

25 SIMPLE TRUTHS ON *Marriage*

KEVIN J. SMITH

The Anima Group

25 Simple Truths on Marriage
All Rights Reserved.
Copyright © 2019 Kevin J. Smith
v2.0

The opinions expressed in this manuscript are solely the opinions of the author and do not represent the opinions or thoughts of the publisher. The author has represented and warranted full ownership and/or legal right to publish all the materials in this book.

This book may not be reproduced, transmitted, or stored in whole or in part by any means, including graphic, electronic, or mechanical without the express written consent of the publisher except in the case of brief quotations embodied in critical articles and reviews.

ISBN: 978-0-578-21009-4

Cover Photo © 2019 www.gettyimages.com. All rights reserved - used with permission.

The Anima Group

PRINTED IN THE UNITED STATES OF AMERICA

Table of Contents

Author's Dedication

I'm just a regular guy.

But, a long time ago I somehow convinced an extraordinary girl to marry me. It was a pretty lousy proposal, not nearly what she deserved, but like she normally does, Julie looked past that moment and saw something bigger and better.

Today, many years after taking our vows, this book is a small gift to my wife, a small thank you for all she has taught me and all we have learned together. There are of course countless things that together make up a marriage that lasts but I have selected a simple twenty-five from the many.

Twenty-five is a number that means something special to us.

I share these simple thoughts with each of you in the hope that it's pages might contain a few ideas that can help your marriage be just a little better, a little happier, a little richer.

Please don't confuse simple with easy, because marriage is anything but easy. I wanted the book to be short because we all have so little time. Sometimes with a simple thought we can redouble our efforts to do the right things day in and day out, building a stronger marriage moment by moment. Nothing is more important than these moments for they are what build a marriage that lasts, that stands the test of time, that stands up to what life throws at us.

Nothing matters more than the journey we take with our spouse, in keeping our vows, in keeping our promise. Nothing else comes close.

To Julie, you taught me everything.

Acknowledgements

I was blessed to be raised in a home with parents that were very much grounded in strong values and dedicated to each other, to a happy home, and to a lasting marriage. Today, my mom and dad are approaching their 60th wedding anniversary. Amazing.

My sincere appreciation and admiration goes to our good friends Matt and Mindy Dalton who founded a Marriage Ministry in order to help marriages through the challenges life brings and in coaching couples to equip them with what is needed to build a marriage that stands the test of time. Their work is so vital and desperately needed.

Something to Remember

Marriage is not just important, it is the single most important thing we will ever do.

More important than friends, more important than the family we grew up with, more important than our parents, more important than any job. Yes, all these things are important. But make no mistake, they don't equal our marriage.

If there is anything in our lives worth working hard for, worth fighting for, worth getting better for, it is our marriage.

If we get anything right in our lives, this is the one thing.

Marriage carries with it a remarkable circle of influences that can't be underestimated. Every marriage touches so many others in so many ways both large and small.

Every marriage is the fabric of our culture. Marriage creates families and families are our future. You might be a family of 2, you and your spouse, or a family of 10, it doesn't matter. Marriage is the fundamental building block of a happy and healthy culture—modeling so much of what makes our world better.

As such a failed marriage has an impact that is difficult to fully appreciate—this influence will carry on for many years, and likely for generations.

A successful marriage is even more powerful than a failed marriage. It fundamentally lays a foundation that brings health and happiness to all the people we touch every day. Far beyond the couple from which this wonderful force springs.

Remember this because there will be days when marriage is hard, when we aren't sure we can go on. But we have to, because it is so important, because so much is at stake.

Keep this in your heart always.

Love

TRUTH #1

*W*e begin with love.

Some time ago the moment came when you knew that this person, your future spouse, was someone special. Unlike anybody you had ever met. At that moment you might not have thought about marriage, but that time would come. Throughout the time that has passed since that first moment, your love was growing and getting stronger. You might not always feel it or be aware of it, but love was growing.

Eventually, that love brought us to an engagement and then the day of our wedding and special vows.

Love has always been there at every step.

Most of you would agree that a lasting and happy marriage is not possible without unconditional love. But what does that really mean? This is the very same question many of us have, but answering this question is not an easy thing.

Part of our challenge is that love has been twisted, diluted and distorted in our world today. The word is thrown around casually, without much thought or attached to much meaning. Young people will say goodbye to a friend with a quick 'I love you' and nobody thinks anything of it.

People in a relationship today start saying 'I love you' after being together for only a short while. This is very much a product of our culture and these same young people simply don't understand in the least what they are saying. They mean no harm, it is innocent enough, but this love does not resemble and should not be confused with what we discover in marriage.

The love that grows in a marriage is one of a kind.

The love of marriage is anything but casual, anything but thoughtless, and is filled with meaning.

Let's go back to our question—what does love really mean? After all, many people don't understand what lies ahead with love at the beginning of a marriage. We know that we are very much in love with our spouse, but when we step into marriage we don't really know what to expect.

We are excited, but a little scared too.

Much is the same, but so much is different and all the good wishes and little talks we had with friends and family, perhaps our mom or dad, could not possibly prepare us for the journey that begins on our wedding day.

One good way to give love meaning is to take on a commitment to love our spouse like we have never loved another person.

Yes, we have loved our parents and we have loved our siblings and other important people in our lives. This idea is not intended to take anything away from the amazing people we have known throughout our lives. But the love we have for our spouse, the love that happens in marriage is different. It just is. It brings us to discover a depth of love that we can only discover in the miracle of marriage.

The spousal relationship is stronger and more sacred than any other relationship on earth.

What has happened before does not matter, only the love that grows following our vows and with every day we spend together. Every morning we wake up next to our spouse brings us new surprises and amazing moments.

To give us a bit more context here, in our desire to better understand love we go back to the beginning of marriage, back to the day of our wedding. On that day, we took our vows and made a promise that we will come to understand is the single most important promise we will ever make.

These vows go something like this:

> *I, take you, to be my (husband/wife). I promise*
> *to be true to you in good times and in bad,*

*in sickness and in health, I will love you and
honor you all the days of my life.*

These vows are unique and only shared on the day of our wedding.
They remain at the heart of our marriage always, and are all about
lasting and growing love, trust, faithfulness and staying together.

Taking another step in answering the question of what love really
means, we will come to appreciate that an unconditional love is
absolutely *selfless* where many of us were all about ourselves before
marriage. I know that I was. Selfish is natural and all that we know
before marriage.

But a day comes in a marriage when we realize that we must choose
between our own happiness and the happiness of our spouse.

*When that day comes, we choose the happiness of our spouse. It's not
hard because we already know the answer.*

We don't know how we got there or why, but we gladly make this
choice because the happiness of our spouse has become so important to us that it now overtakes all our own selfish needs.

We are able to leave that stuff from our past behind. In so many
ways, our spouse and our marriage have saved us from our weak
and selfish selves.

Now, as our marriage grows it will become more common for you
and your spouse to want the same thing and to be very much on
the same page. But when that is not possible, we choose to set our
own feelings aside and choose what we know will make our spouse
happy.

This is an important point in a marriage and it comes at a different time for all of us, but this simple thing, this simple behavior says so much. This is a sign that our love has grown and has become a selfless love that is so important in a marriage. In virtually every way, this selfless love of marriage is nothing like the love we thought we knew before the day of our wedding.

This new sense of selflessness is one of our little miracles—a truly wonderful thing in a marriage as we will discuss time and time again.

So that means we have reached a point where we understand fully that we love our spouse like we have never loved another person, and we willingly choose their needs and their happiness over our own.

Even more remarkably, we are happy to do this.

Love prepares us for the tough times by weaving a fabric of trust and respect which binds us to our spouse and enables us to enjoy the best of times and to carry us through the hardest of times.

In our culture today, people struggle with making promises. The reasons for this are many, but we simply live in a 'me-first' world that is less about commitment and more about immediate gratification. This has been nurtured by a culture that is thoroughly confused and distracted. A culture without direction and increasingly lacking a soul.

Real love is fundamentally different. True love wants to make a promise and to keep a promise. It pulls us in a direction that is very much the opposite of popular culture.

Love desires to take a vow.

A lasting vow is all but impossible with shallow or selfish love. The deeper and stronger our love, the more we desire to take a vow, to make a promise and then to keep the promise every day.

These vows, and the love that carries them forward in our marriage holds the promise that we will never be alone. That the trials of life will not be faced alone. This is a powerful part of marriage.

While a strong marriage has an element that is steady and dependable, marriage can bring us surprises too. Love never stops changing. It is different for all of us and it can be a whisper, or it can be utterly overpowering and knock us to our knees.

We call on love to help us when we have a day that is so hard we don't know what to do and we feel small and helpless. And, we thank love for it's grace and miracle when we have a day that is absolutely perfect.

A happy marriage is carried by the strength of Love, and when we are frustrated or mad or tired, take a moment and close your eyes and think about the very best of your wife or husband and what you love most about them. When was the first time we felt a flutter in our stomach and knew they were special? What do you love most about them?

This reflection softens our heart when we need a little help and little things matter. The miracle of Love is as much about the little things as it is about the big things.

Prayer

TRUTH #2

*P*rayer is a wonderful and powerful secret weapon in our marriage.

Prayer is unique as a force that can make everything that is good in a marriage even better, and a place to turn when we need help in overcoming the challenges that come our way.

Attacks on our marriage can come from anywhere at any time. When these attacks come, we will fight for our marriage and we will use prayer as one of our weapons. We just can't fight this battle alone. But with our spouse by our side and with prayer we can overcome any force of bad that threatens us.

In a world where so many people feel compelled to understand and shout about the limits of anything and everything—prayer is the rare exception in that it truly has no limits.

Prayer can be there to lift us up, when life feels overwhelming and we feel so small and helpless.

Prayer works when nothing else can.

A prayer might be a few seconds or it might be a one-hour service, or a celebration or mass, or a weekend retreat. All of this is ok. Even a few seconds of prayer can be a powerful force and change your day.

Regardless of your faith, pray *for* your spouse and *with* your spouse.

Try to pray every day, whether it be a few seconds, a few minutes or more. When you do pray, always remember to pray for your spouse and for your marriage.

Praying daily is a good practice that I highly recommend and one you will never regret.

When we like to describe and quantify the downside of everything, prayer is something that has no downside.

Julie and I are Catholic, but we have good friends of many faiths— Jewish, Mormon, Baptist, Muslim, Hindu, Presbyterian, Lutheran, and much more.

All faiths are wonderful and unique.

The key here is the element of prayer and faith in a successful marriage. It simply can't be underestimated.

A great time to pray is when you first open your eyes in the morning. The day is fresh and you have a moment of silence before the demands of today carry us away. Pray for your spouse, for your marriage, and for the needs of your family. Give thanks every chance you get and ask for the help you need.

If you don't pray today or don't know how to pray but want to get started, it's best to keep it simple. If you are not sure how this goes, I recommend something like this:

> *Thank you Lord for my countless blessings.*
> *Thank you for [recognize a few good things in your life]*
> *Thank you for my wife/husband, they are my greatest gift.*
> *Grant our marriage the strength we need every day.*
> *I humbly ask You to help me to be the best wife/husband I can.*
> *Please grant these wishes [special intentions for today].*
> *Although I'm not worthy of any request, please hear these prayers today.*
> *Amen.*

Begin with giving thanks and remember that prayer is not just about asking for what we need at the moment. Yes, that is part of prayer but giving thanks for the wonderful gifts we receive every day has an equal, perhaps greater place in prayer.

If it can help, take this simple suggested prayer and make it your own. Prayer should be personal, honest and humble. After all, our God already knows what you have and what you need. No need for long and complicated prayers. No need to negotiate.

The key is to just pray. Any prayer makes a big difference.

What you'll likely discover is that you naturally begin to look forward to your prayer time and it won't be a chore, or something to be delayed or avoided, but rather a treat, a comfort. You might already be there and that is great because many of you are. If not, that is ok too and I hope you are able to discover this amazing sense of peace and fulfillment.

Marriages with a strong element of faith, a marriage that includes prayer, is more likely to be a happy marriage and a marriage that lasts.

There is no more powerful place to share prayer than within the spousal relationship—this amazing place that is unlike any other.

But we are all on our own journey and if you don't currently make prayer a part of your life, consider doing it now. Suggest it to your spouse and talk about it. They might very well have this on their heart too and be ready to start. It is not hard to find a few minutes in your day.

Praying when you are alone is in itself a wonderful thing. Praying with your spouse is a hundred times better. This power of together magnifies all that is good about prayer.

Whether you are fully content with your marriage and simply looking for new ways to grow, or you are struggling with your marriage and searching for a new path to make your marriage stronger, make prayer a part of this commitment.

You can't do this alone.

I can't begin to imagine facing the challenges, decisions, setbacks, joys, and triumphs of both marriage and life without prayer. We are so small and prayer helps us to find our way and face what can seem so hard and so big.

As an added bonus, prayer cultivates love for our spouse and our sense of humility. Many of the most meaningful insights of my life have come through prayer. I'm both amazed by how stupid I can be, and how prayer can then lift me up and show me things that I would never see on my own.

Saint Augustine said it well:

'Pray as though everything depended on God. Work as though everything depended on you'.

Wise words to live by.

Humility

TRUTH #3

*I*n a world that is increasingly frenzied, selfish, and distracted, humility is often missing.

This wonderful quality is overlooked when we need it more than ever in life and certainly in our marriage.

Think for a moment about the most humble people you know—do you admire them? Are they strong? Are they someone you trust? Are they someone you like? Are they dependable? The answer to all these questions is likely yes.

Certainly, humility as wonderful as it can be, is not a natural mindset for most people. We are wired to survive, to be selfish, to seek our own happiness. But humility calls us to go down a different path.

It could be that the first time we consider humility is when we take our marriage vows because these vows are so much <u>not about you</u>.

Our vows are all about what we are together and for one another, about the unity of our marriage.

It won't happen overnight, but the day we take our vows should be the beginning of a transformation in our thinking, a move from any lingering ego and selfishness to a focus on sharing and the happiness of our spouse over our own happiness.

Ego, pride and arrogance are dangerous emotions that have no place in a marriage. These things are poison to our vows.

Many of us carry some of this with us going into our marriage. But we need to just leave these behind and let any of these things we are clinging to fade away. Our spouse is worth it.

Humility naturally creates a sense of selflessness and brings a vital balance to our marriage. Growing humility can neutralize these poisonous and selfish emotions like nothing else can. Humility is a powerful medicine for our soul and those things that can harm our marriage.

Part of marriage is understanding and then believing, and then acting on the idea that it's not about you. Let me say that again,

it's not about you.

It's about the marriage and your wonderful spouse.

The power of humility and selflessness is the more we give our spouse, the more they will want to give back to us.

Sometimes it's not easy to give first, but it will always come back to us as another remarkable gift only marriage can give.

This commitment to humility then reinforces one of our key goals in marriage which is to put the happiness of your spouse before your own. This is another thing we discussed in the chapter on love and are reminded yet again of the connection between love and humility.

Just remember that sometimes we need to be the first to be selfless, and sometimes we might need to do this more than once, maybe a hundred times, but then when it does come back to us it is an amazing thing to behold. And, it will come back to us.

Commit to be first in being selfless, and you won't regret it.

Another element of humility is understanding, and really believing, that when we accomplish something great in our marriage individually, the credit should always go to your spouse and to the marriage. This sense of unity reinforces many things, including just how much we owe to our spouse for everything that we are today and everything we will be.

Always give credit to your spouse when you are better than you were before, when you win, when you grow.

It's not about you.

There is no room for ego in a successful marriage. This is a foolish pursuit and one that will grow many problems. Of course, for some people this will take some work because you might have a bit of an ego coming into the marriage. I know that I did.

But your spouse is worth getting better, so just commit to taming your ego over time. It won't happen in a day or a week, but something you can work on over time and push the ego down. Let humility become the bigger of the two.

Your spouse will notice, and they are likely to take on the same commitment.

Humility is a great reminder, and one that can always bring us back to our center—the fundamental truth that marriage is not about me. It is about us, it is about our wonderful spouse. Put the marriage and our spouse first and so many things fall into place.

Be just a little more humble, a little less selfish every day and it will make a big difference in your journey.

Your spouse will notice and they will love you even more for it.

Patience

TRUTH #4

*I*f anything is worthy of our patience, it's marriage. Start here.

Patience, love and humility are closely linked. This is one example of a few of our vital marriage triunes*—patience with our spouse will strengthen our love for each other, and the commitment to this patience will further deepen our love and enhance our humility. Even those of us that are not naturally patient, should commit to developing this as a gift in our marriage. Like so many other wonderful gifts in our marriage, when we commit to patience with our spouse, a type of patience we have never provided to any other person in our lives, it will be returned to us.

[*] credit goes to Matt Dalton from whom I borrowed this wonderful word.

This is another essential example of something that is not easy, perhaps not natural, but our spouse needs this from us and we should be up to the challenge.

Our spouse will make mistakes and that's ok because we will too. Oh goodness we will too. When that time comes, we hope our spouse will be patient and forgiving in kind. They will.

Please be patient with me, and I will be patient with you.

Even when we are fundamentally impatient with all others, we can reach deep inside ourselves and find patience for our spouse. This might take some time and will certainly take some effort, but they are worth it. More-so than anybody else.

This is another reminder of the miracle of the spousal relationship and how it can elevate us to exceed what we have ever done before.

You are not perfect and when you make mistakes your spouse will love you just the same. You then give this wonderful gift of patience back to your spouse.

There is another important relationship here, another dimension to patience, and that is the patience with ourselves. We commit to working hard on improving our own shortcomings and in being patient with ourselves while this ongoing improvement occurs, just as we are with our spouse. If we are impatient with ourselves, this turns into frustration and anger and this then spills over into and undermines our patience with our spouse.

For a great insight on this we consider the words of Saint Francis de

Sales: 'Have patience with all things, but chiefly have patience with yourself. Do not lose courage in considering your own imperfections but instantly set about remedying them, every day begin the task anew'.

Normally our spouse will be understanding when we are open about trying to improve in any one of the things we are working on, and it just takes some time. Communicating that we are trying to improve, is likely to help with the patience thing. Communicate and be open and that will really help. They know us better than anybody.

It's a great thing to discuss, especially in the midst of a disagreement or a full-out argument. It can even be a way to get past the argument, simply acknowledging you need to be better with that particular thing and to please be patient.

Avoid being stubborn and prideful.

This combination has hurt as many marriages as any other single thing I know. And normally, when we dig in and choose to be stubborn or prideful, it's about something small. Something stupid in the light of day. Very likely something that is not worth the wasted time of an argument.

Patience does not come naturally to many of us, but our spouse is worth it. Maybe, just maybe, our spouse is the only person on this earth we are willing or able to be patient with.

That's ok. It's a start and something to build on.

By the way, they <u>are</u> worth it. Make no mistake. Fight hard to give them this gift.

Patience can sometimes be born in the marriage because we work hard at making the marriage better, but with some degree of new-found patience this can then extend into other parts of our lives.

Patience in the workplace can serve us well, patience with family ditto, patience with kids for sure, patience is just a powerful behavior to role model.

When working on patience, it helps to step out of ourselves and remember how good it feels when somebody else is patient with us.

It's a wonderful thing to be on the right side of patience so this is a good exercise to help us take a moment and commit to being just a little better.

Beyond patience, this is a good practice for many things in marriage—take a step back and think for just a few seconds about how it feels to be on the other side.

Remember, it's not about you.

Honesty

TRUTH #5

*T*his is a big one.

Big because it is so important, and at the same time a struggle for many.

Honesty is an issue at some stage in virtually every marriage. Like many big things, the best way to get better with honesty is by taking small steps. Just getting a little better every day, every month, every year. Make it a priority, make it a focus, put it on the short list of the things you will work on for your spouse and for your marriage.

What we will learn over time is that it's just best to be honest. From the get-go. Complete honesty is very empowering, very simple, very consistent.

The truth is the only version of any single thing that is perfectly clear.

Complete honesty earns trust, earns respect. If anybody in our lives is deserving of our complete honesty, it's our spouse. For many, the only person they have ever been completely honest with is their spouse and that is ok. They deserve our best after all.

Little lies might seem convenient or even necessary in the moment but this is a dangerous trap. It is very likely our spouse already knows the truth or will soon, and little lies weaken our trust and weaken our marriage.

Little lies are a poison.

Remember, our spouse knows us better than anybody and they probably know the moment we tell a little lie or a big lie—they will know that something is not quite right. If not then, they will know the truth soon enough.

The truth has a way of coming out. Always. The truth is unstoppable.

So, a little lie is not worth it. I promise you, it's just not worth it.

There are a few things that must exist in a successful marriage and trust is one. So much becomes possible with trust, and so much becomes all but impossible when trust does not exist.

Honesty starts with you.

Be honest with yourself—that's the first step to getting better about being honest with your spouse. That comes next, but it starts with looking yourself in the mirror and being absolutely honest about what we are and what we are not.

Make no mistake, being honest with ourselves is not easy. But, it is important, even vital to your marriage. It is a personal revelation.

There is no better time to leave bad habits behind than when we take the vows of marriage. These vows bring with them a commitment to be better for our spouse than we could be ever be for ourselves. This is a powerful idea—when it was just me, I did many things that were selfish or convenient or easy.

But now, our marriage calls me to be better than I could ever be on my own.

Honesty is a great example of a bad habit we can leave behind. Yes, being reckless with the truth is simply a bad habit. Once started, it becomes how we act and how we think.

So, now you should commit to being completely honest with your spouse. This supports and then helps to purify the spousal relationship.

It is amazing how liberating being completely honest really is. It is so simple, just tell the truth every time, the first time. This is another case of role modeling the right behavior for the marriage and it can come from either spouse.

Setting a standard of honesty then creates a natural pull for your spouse to take on the same commitment. Then, both of you being completely honest all the time, well that is really something.

All of us are naturally drawn to honesty. We respect and admire people that are honest and direct. We just know this is right. The remarkable thing about honesty is that it's completely under our control.

There are many things we can't control, but we are the masters of our own honesty.

A marriage can be a great starting point for improved honesty, and when this carries over into the rest of our life it only gets better. There is no real downside to honesty—it helps us in every aspect of our life.

Honesty is a wonderful force for good and a remarkable gift to your spouse.

So, what are we waiting for?

Affection

TRUTH #6

A little tenderness is a wonderful thing to be part of and to behold.

Affection can be a small touch, holding hands when you are walking with your spouse, sitting close to each other at a restaurant, or just a hug. A kiss on the cheek. All of this is simple and perfect. It sends a message that we are very much in love with our spouse. Our world needs more of this.

> *A reminder of how much we need them.*
> *A reminder of how happy we are with them.*
> *A reminder they are the most important person in our life.*

This is part of the communication that happens every day. Our words and our actions reinforce everything our spouse needs to know from us. When what we say and what we do go together, it's a wonderful thing.

Affection is an important reminder of our love, of our commitment, of our patience.

Another wonderful thing about affection is the message it sends to others. They will notice the affection we share with our spouse. Today, there seems to be a common stereotype that the affection of married couples fades over time.

We can't let that happen—if anything, the feelings and affection of a healthy marriage grow over time. That's why a little tenderness and affection is such a powerful thing. It's an important message to the people around us, the people we know and the people we don't know, of how much we love them, how important they are to us, how much we enjoy just being together.

The little things, as we are reminded over and over again, mean so much in a happy marriage. These reminders are for our spouse, and for our family, our friends and everybody in our lives.

Smile. A smile warms our heart and lifts the spirits of all the people around us. Never underestimate a smile. When you feel yourself getting frustrated or mad, just take a deep breath and smile. Slow everything down for a moment.

Affection slows down the crazy motion of the day and brings us closer together for just a minute.

Don't underestimate those moments, they are a magical glue for our marriage. The moments of affection are another needle that weave the fabric of love, of trust, of commitment.

Affection is a wonderful way to communicate without saying anything.

What is your first reaction when you see a couple walking along hold-ing hands? Like most people, you probably think that is really cool.

You think those people are happy. They are very much in love. And that reaction is based on a very simple thing, a bit of affection.

Don't allow the distance to grow between you and your spouse. Stay close, we want to feel their warmth, to feel the comfort of being close. I know that Julie always smells great, and I try to get as close as I can to her every chance I get. How I smell, well that is a different story…

Never underestimate the power of a hug, the power of a little kiss on the cheek. This is the good stuff.

There are so many little things we can do during the day that show a little tenderness. Open a door. Help carry something. Take the bags from your spouse when you are shopping and make their load a little lighter. Let your spouse go before you in line. Offer your spouse a helping hand when you are going down stairs. Pull the chair out for your spouse when you're having a meal out. All these little things matter.

Every day should include a little affection for our spouse. Where there is affection there is love and respect. They always go together and this creates a powerful circle of affirmation for the vows we took on the day we were married. Our affection and our tender-ness is a simple way to renew our vows and to renew them bit by bit every day. Without saying a word.

All of this really means that we love them more than ever and love them more every day.

Apology

TRUTH #7

A sincere apology is a simple and wonderful thing in a marriage. Who doesn't like a sincere apology? I can't think of any single thing that can more quickly and more completely stop an argument that is building like a storm, than a sincere apology.

This is another secret weapon in our marriage.

An apology is remarkably disarming and can turn everything around in an instant.

Remember, we are talking about a truly sincere apology.

A lousy apology on the other hand might actually make things worse. Just don't do that.

This does not come naturally to many people. Perhaps our parents didn't role model this behavior when we were young, maybe because we are just stubborn, maybe because we just hate to admit we made a mistake.

Sound familiar?

In the end, it doesn't matter where you have come from or where you are today. Learn to appreciate the importance of apologizing in your marriage and don't hesitate to apologize first. This is not a time for keeping score. If you are always the first to apologize, that is great and just keep doing it.

The reality is that if we've had a disagreement with our spouse, if we have had an argument, big or small, with lots of anger or just a little anger, it is very likely we have contributed to it in some way.

It really helps to realize that any disagreement likely comes from mistakes made by both you and your spouse. Rarely if ever does you or your wonderful wife or husband carry a full 100% of the responsibility when things go bad. Yes, it's true and it helps to remember this.

> *The best apology is simple and direct. 'I'm very sorry that I…'.*
> *'I hate to argue with you, so please accept my apology…'*
> *'Let's not waste another minute of our day, and I promise that I will try to do better next time…'*
> *'I love you so much, and I'm very sorry that I did that…'*
> *'I know how much you dislike it when I…. and I'm so sorry I did that again. That was really stupid of me and I will try harder next time…'*

You get the idea.

It helps to recognize if we are making a mistake that we've made in the past, doing something that is sensitive to our spouse, something we know they feel strongly about.

We are human, some of us more so than others, and we are going to make mistakes. So, when that happens we need to recognize it and the sooner the better. Don't let things get worse, it is far better to apologize quickly so things can get better before they get much worse.

By the way, an apology that includes a disclaimer or a footnote doesn't really work.

This is not a time to try to make a case for what you did not being all that bad.

Yes, we all have the urge to do this and it's natural. But, leave that urge behind and this is a time for being sincere, for stepping up to the mistakes you've made, and for committing to doing better next time.

All in, no holding back.

Most disagreements are avoidable, so we all need to pay attention to the things that happen before an argument and work hard at keeping the argument from taking flight the next time. Prevention is a wonderful thing and is very doable if we just pay attention. Pay attention to the warning signs.

'I can see that you are getting upset, so please let me make this better before we both end up mad...'

We normally have a pretty good idea of when our spouse is beginning to get mad about something, so pay attention to those signs whatever they might be and do what we can to turn things around. Think of this as the first phase of an argument and apologizing in this first phase is way better than trying to take this on later.

Don't let the argument escalate.

Even if you are not sure your spouse is getting mad about something, it's best to ask right way and to apologize if necessary.

The willingness to apologize sincerely is just a lifestyle thing we should all commit to in a marriage. Another good habit.

Even if we have never apologized in our life previously, this is another dimension that builds and protects the spousal relationship. Another brick in our foundation.

The only real barrier to an apology is our own selfish pride, and it's a wonderful gift we can give to our spouse that will help our marriage so much over time.

Back to the role modeling thing, we can both role model this to our spouse and if you have children, this is a wonderful thing to role model for your kids as they inevitably take forward into their marriage the behaviors we as parents display every day in our marriage. This is a timeless gift we can give our kids for their future spouse—train them to apologize.

We can also role model this behavior to our married friends. Do you have any friends that are struggling with their marriage?

Many of us do, and this could help the circle of people we touch in our lives.

Pass it on and they will thank you some day.

Compromise

TRUTH #8

*W*hether we realize it or not, there is a lot of healthy compromise that is necessary and practical in a marriage. The key here is to find a middle ground when necessary and then move forward together.

When we do this right, both you and your spouse will get what you want and feel good about it.

We don't always agree with our spouse and in that moment, we have the opportunity to find a solution that works for both of us. This is far better than getting stuck and both walking away disappointed.

There is no need to go down that path.

This is simply a practical and natural thing. With the many

decisions we make every day in marriage, and some days it feels like there are thousands of these, it is just not possible to always be in 100% agreement with your spouse.

It could be about running errands, paying bills, about what our plans should be for the evening, about an upcoming family event, how to spend a holiday, a consequence for one of the kids, it could be any one of the many things we deal with every day.

See any small gap between what you and your spouse prefer, when faced with the countless decisions we make day in and day out, as an opportunity to close that gap with a little creative negotiating.

It could be as simple as 'how about you pick the move tonight, and I get to pick it the next time?'. Note that you are giving up the first-round draft pick, which is a gracious thing to do. Every little concession like this makes a difference.

Resist the temptation to put yourself first, resist the urge to be stubborn or selfish, these emotions are a fools errand. Just don't do it.

Be flexible. Mercy me is flexible a wonderful thing in a marriage.

This is especially important over time, as the years pass. Don't just be flexible, *stay* flexible. If anything, try to be more flexible as the years pass so you don't become part of that stereotype of couples growing apart over time.

Let your spouse pick, and then be happy about what they pick. This just makes everything a lot easier for everybody. And, if you catch yourself slipping back into being stubborn or selfish, just stop and pull yourself up again.

Not naturally a flexible person? A strong-willed person accustomed to getting what they want? Ok, you are not alone, we all have a streak of this in us, but understand how this mindset is not a good thing for our marriage. Your spouse is worthy of your best, better than you have ever been.

I'm confident you can do it because you are reading this book which means you are willing to learn, willing to take the time to get better, willing to hear new ideas.

Congratulations, that is exactly how we grow and get better.

I don't expect you to put all twenty-five truths into action immediately but if you take away from the book just a couple of the truths to focus on then I'm thrilled and honored to have helped. This idea of compromise and playful negotiating might be helpful.

Getting just a little better every day or every week is a great way to improve. We all have our little battles, our issues that we carry with us that we need to overcome. This is what makes us human and our spouses likely already know every one of these challenges we carry with us and it's ok.

Sharing our weaknesses, our challenges and our insecurities with our spouses is one of the little miracles of marriage. It's very likely that our spouse knows us better than anybody and so our wonderful bond grows even stronger. They know everything about us, our strengths and our weaknesses and our issues and everything else. And it is all ok. We love each other at our best and we love each other at our worst.

Compromise with a smile, and give your spouse a little win every chance you get. They will notice and that good deed will come back to you.

The bottom line is turning an impasse, or a disagreement that's going in the wrong direction into something good. I'm convinced that in 99% of the cases, we can find a compromise on virtually any topic, and create a plan that both you and your spouse will feel good about.

This is more than just another thing, this is one of the pillars of a healthy marriage. No two people agree all the time.

So, the big thing becomes how we take the next steps and our willingness to be flexible and patient in finding an outcome we both feel pretty good about.

It's there, we just need to find it.

Fitness

TRUTH #9

*F*itness contributes to a healthy lifestyle, and as such it has a place in a healthy marriage. Fitness is somewhat unique in that exercise is a fun activity you can share with your spouse and while we're at it, it gives us a great time to just be together and talk about stuff we normally don't have time to talk about.

As an extension to exercise, healthy eating is important to our long-term health as well as our overall fitness and this is another thing we can do together. It's not easy if you or your spouse are trying to eat healthier and the other is not on-board.

This makes everything more complicated, and just harder.

But if you and your spouse commit to exercising regularly and eating healthier then you are working as a team and as a team it is much more likely you will stick with it.

Remember, this is an investment in your health which then translates into an investment in your marriage. Good health brings energy, good health encourages optimism, good health brings strength, good health helps to ensure you are here far into the future for your spouse.

As we age, a commitment to exercise and to eating good food makes a big difference. It is hard to sustain a happy marriage in poor health.

Everything is harder if you feel bad.

However, you and your spouse being in good health equips you with a robust body with which you can face the challenges of life with your spouse.

There is something about exercise that clears our head, that brings us new ideas.

Hard exercise is even better.

There is something about a great meal with clean and healthy food that brings us a sense of contentment and replenishment.

A sense of doing the right thing for our overall health and well-being. Good and clean food every day brings so many health benefits.

Remember that our body is the world's most advanced machine so when we give it the right fuel, everything works better.

We are stronger for the little physical things that come our way every day. I'm convinced that good food helps us think better too. Try it and you will be surprised.

Eating better starts with the next meal. Just take baby steps and you will likely notice you feel better and have more energy. This then brings us encouragement to continue our commitment to eating better, to eating the best available food. A little more progress then makes us more determined.

It really helps when you see results.

When exercising, it doesn't really matter what you do, just do something.

It could be a short walk, a longer hike, a bike ride, lifting weights, mowing the yard, rock climbing, cross fit, skating, playing a sport together, chopping wood, or any one of a hundred different things.

Just don't do something you hate. If you don't like it, you won't keep doing it so find something you enjoy.

All that matters is to find what works for you and to make time to exercise, and then do it together whenever possible. Sometimes it just won't work to do it together, but when it is possible find the time to exercise as a team. This is better than the two of you always doing your own thing.

Maybe you and your spouse exercise separately during the week because of work schedules, commutes, or the location of your offices. That's ok, but try to do an exercise session together on the weekend. Maybe a long one, and it could be followed by breakfast or something fun. Maybe a stop at a favorite coffee shop, or smoothie place.

If either you or your spouse exercises regularly and the other doesn't currently do that, then surprise your spouse and join in.

They will like the surprise and will be happy to spend the time together.

How good is that?

Better still, if both of you are not exercising but you have both agreed this is a goal, then make it happen. Get started together. It is so much easier to do something together versus going at it alone.

Make the time, the other stuff can wait. This is a gift to your health and to your marriage and like so many other things we will discuss throughout the book it can be something you could not do for yourself but you can do for your spouse.

Eating better is not just a single thing, it is a natural complement to exercise. Good food will give you energy and strength for your exercise. Improved stamina will help with other parts of your life too. More stamina will help with your job, it will help with your hobbies.

Good food will improve your exercise and exercise will grow your bodies desire for clean food. It is a powerful pair of good forces and this builds a healthy lifestyle.

Trying to lose a few pounds? Many of us are, so make it a fun thing with your spouse. You can do together what is really hard on your own.

Both of you will appreciate looking better and feeling better. Be sure to compliment your spouse when they do make progress and let them know they look great.

Keep it fun and keep it simple. Keep the goals for dropping a few pounds reasonable and encourage one another. Every pound makes a difference and makes it easier to lose the next pound.

You will discover that your body adapts every day and will give you a little more strength to exercise, and it will ask you for better food.

Less of the bad stuff and more of the good stuff.

To help organize my own eating over the years, I've made a list of the top 10 foods to avoid and the top 10 foods to enjoy and I will share my lists with you and hope that it helps a little:

TOP 10 FOODS TO AVOID:

1. Soft drinks. Especially diet drinks. All-natural sodas are much better.
2. Artificial colors, sweeteners and preservatives. Very bad stuff.
3. Cheese and fatty dairy. Ok for kids, not for adults.
4. Deep fried foods. Just don't do it.
5. Fatty meats. Stay clear of sausages and fatty lunch meats.
6. Sugar and high fructose corn syrup. They are everywhere.
7. Crackers, cakes and cookies. No hydrogenated oils.
8. Rich sauces and dressings. Lots of bad stuff can hide there.
9. Bleached flour breads and rolls. Love bread? Eat whole grain, natural, organic breads with lots of fiber.
10. Any commercial food that's highly processed with a long list of ingredients you don't recognize. Read the labels on everything.

Top 10 foods to enjoy:

1. Fresh fruit. Blueberries, blackberries, cranberries and apples are great.

2. Oatmeal and porridge. Eat a good breakfast.

3. Pistachios, macadamia nuts and walnuts. A great snack.

4. Olive oil and garlic. Fantastic to cook with.

5. Fresh vegetables. Broccoli, spinach and peppers are favorites.

6. Properly sourced, low mercury fish. Salmon, tuna, halibut are good choices.

7. Lean, organic meats. Invest in organic meats and keep portions small.

8. Dark chocolate. A perfect treat.

9. Guacamole and hummus are healthy snacks or sides.

10. Whole grain, high fiber, organic breads.

This is not a book about nutrition and food so we will leave it there.

But in raising the subject I thought it would help to provide a little more detail on how you can eat better if you don't already have a plan in place. Some of you will have already done the homework and be working on this now.

My experience has been that eating good, clean and natural food is more important than strictly counting calories. Keep portion sizes reasonable.

Eat the right foods, avoid bad foods, eat a lighter dinner, start with a good breakfast, have a couple of healthy snacks during the day so you don't get too hungry, and you will see a big change in how you look and how you feel. An accurate scale can help you monitor progress. Not dropping the pounds you want? Reduce your intake a little for two weeks and reassess. Everybody is different so learn what works and what does not work for you and learn to appreciate the remarkable adjustments and adaptations our bodies can make.

Our bodies can do amazing things if we just give it a little help.

Fast weight loss is not healthy so don't go crazy.

Exercise has a unique ability to peel back a lot of the daily life stuff that clouds our thinking. I know that my wife and I have solved a lot of problems and hatched a lot of great ideas on our bike rides, walks or hikes. It's just a time when we focus on being together and clear our heads for a little while and have a chance to talk things through. We don't get interrupted every two minutes for one reason or another. Amazing.

Oh yea, put the phones away for a little while too.

The idea of *team* in your marriage is a great thing, and the combination of exercise and healthy eating are just another case of doing something together that is healthy and good.

A fit lifestyle makes us better together and for each other.

When the body is hurt, broken or ailing it impacts the mind and the heart. But when the body is strong and vibrant, the mind works better and so does the heart. Feelings are stronger and more vivid. Our senses are at their best too.

Everything is more clear.

When we improve our overall fitness together it also means we can give each other encouragement when we get discouraged and frustrated.

This teamwork on fitness, like many other things in our marriage, makes it more likely we are successful in accomplishing our goals, and then what do we do?

Exactly, we celebrate!

Communication

TRUTH #10

$\mathcal{W}$e are constantly communicating in our marriage, whether we realize it or not.

The spoken word, body language, expressions, and our actions to name a few. Yes, don't forget about *what we do* because those actions might be the most important communication of all.

Words are important and words can nurture or can hurt equally, but they are temporary and only hang in the air for a moment.

It's best to both communicate verbally what needs to be said, and to then back it up with our actions. Actions last. If these things are not in synch, our spouse will be confused and with good cause. But when our words and our actions are in synch, when they are communicating the same thing, well that is really something.

Mixed messages are confusing, they are upsetting, and they steal our energy and our trust. Don't let this creep into your marriage.

The truly lasting impressions are often the things we do, the actions we take, the things we do every day. And don't forget that the little things we do are really important.

Doing a small chore to save your spouse some time, leaving a little note in the kitchen or bathroom, sending a quick text during the day, just saying 'I love you' when your spouse is having a tough day. This is the good stuff, and what we remember.

All of this helps and weaves the fabric that makes our marriage strong. I like to keep things simple, and a simple 'you look great today', or 'I really missed you while I was at work', or any one of a hundred nice little comments are appreciated.

Who doesn't like to hear nice things?

We all love a kind word, so remember to give as good as we get.

Double down on the important things. It's just not enough to say a kind word. Yes, that is great but is just a start. Then, back it up with actions during the day, and tomorrow, and the day after.

Your spouse will notice and will remember.

Another thing that should not be underestimated is body language. Be aware of your body language when you and your spouse are discussing something that has the potential to escalate into a disagreement and then into an all-out argument. This makes a big difference.

Be aware of the look on your face, your posture, all the things we notice when talking to someone.

Your body language should say 'I'm listening', or 'I'm interested in what you have to say', or 'this is important to me', or 'I'm open to discussing this and finding a solution'. Some discussions go bad within the first few minutes because our body language is all wrong.

Once again it pays to remember that our spouse knows us better than anybody and will know right away what we are thinking.

Heck, they might know what we are thinking before we do.

So, make it a point to have a clear mind and to support that with good body language whenever you and your spouse navigate into a discussion that has the potential to go bad. You know, stuff like money, family events, parents, jobs. The stuff that ninety percent of our arguments are about.

Preventing an argument is a far better strategy than trying to navigate out of one once it had started. It's way better to just not get to that point.

Good thoughts, good actions, good body language, and good words.

Not a bad thing to remember my friends. This is the stuff that nurtures a happy marriage and chips away at an unhappy marriage.

This is another case of forming a good habit versus forming a bad habit. Work hard at being a better communicator and it will pay back to us in our marriage over time.

You will see a difference.

Hobbies

TRUTH #11

*L*ife is fuller, richer, and just plain more fun when we enjoy and invest time in our hobbies. This brings a nice balance to our lives. A good outlet that is healthy.

Most of us have hobbies and it could be anything. The stuff we do that we enjoy, that makes us excited, that we look forward to on the weekend, that we look forward to as part of a vacation.

And let's be clear—it doesn't really matter what these are, just that we recognize that investing time in our passions and those of our spouse is healthy, fun and fulfilling.

A fuller life lived, is a happier life and a happier marriage. Hobbies that intersect with those of our spouse are even better. And, a combination of hobbies that our spouse might not share, with hobbies we can share with our spouse is fine too. This just means we need to do a little planning on how we spend our time because our hobbies should not pull us away from our spouse too much.

Our hobbies can lift us up, keep life interesting, and help steer us away from the ruts that are so common with the ups and downs life will bring us.

I like the idea of working hard and then playing hard. This is a simple thing to keep in mind and a good way to live.

So, the playing hard brings us back to our hobbies and the important role they have.

These things can regulate each other, meaning that if we are working hard but not playing hard, that is a problem, and if we are playing hard but not working hard, that creates another set of problems. But, if we are both working hard and playing hard, life is likely to be good, to be healthy, to be successful. Always mind this balance.

What is your favorite hobby? What does your spouse enjoy doing with their free time? I'm sure you know the answer to both questions.

Here are a couple more questions; how supportive are you of your spouse's hobbies? How supportive are they of yours? The thing we need to understand is that two married people might have much in common and likely do, but their hobbies might not be the same. Your spouse might enjoy fly fishing, or golf, or traveling. You might enjoy cooking, painting, reading, photography or pottery. Great, these are all good because there are no wrong answers here.

What we need to create is a sense of support for each other. Make time to do what we enjoy. Share those experiences when we can. There might be a bit of negotiating here that works well. You pick the activity in the morning and your spouse picks the evening activity.

Take a hike in the morning and go to a museum that evening. The combinations are endless.

The spousal relationship is not just spiritual, not just about battles of morality and honesty. There needs to be fun too, and our hobbies bring us some fun.

To support your spouse, to take an interest in what your spouse enjoys so much, and to learn something about it. Then, the two of you have more to discuss, and some stuff that is fun to talk about is just a bonus.

Taking this a step further, encourage your spouse to chase their passions (within reason of course). They will be happier, they will appreciate the support, and are likely to return the favor.

There is some caution in order here because sometimes our passions can begin to consume us. After all, they are by definition something we enjoy and something we feel strongly about and with that in mind, sometimes our spouse will need to reel us in a bit.

A healthy balance is good in all things, moderation if you will, and if we start to go too far then we need to take a pause and reassess how we are spending our time. And the day might come when we return the favor and help remind our spouse of the balance and moderation we need to find in all things.

This is all part of the wonderful circle of our daily lives that our spouse is best qualified to help us navigate, enjoy and repeat.

Charity

TRUTH #12

A number of things we do in our daily lives say a lot about our character, a lot about our values. It is important to realize that every action we take sends a message to all those around us.

We can call this leading, role modeling or witnessing. In any case, doing the right things have many implications and impacts to others.

Think of this as a chain reaction of sorts that runs through our circle of family, friends and associates.

Likewise, doing what we can now call or can later call the wrong things, has an equally extensive set of consequences and impacts. Never underestimate the impact of our actions to our spouse and all those in our circle. The circles of influences in our lives are remarkable.

Being generous with our time and resource is not an easy thing for some, but it is important. Important in that we help others, and at the same time do a small part in making the world a better place.

Never underestimate the impact being generous can have on others.

Both those we share with directly, but also those people otherwise involved in the sharing chain, and those that witness us making this commitment and performing a wonderful service.

In our marriage we should commit to being generous, commit to charity as a priority. This is something we can share and a common value that can be created in our marriage that then becomes a fundamental element of our lifestyle.

Maybe you or your spouse are not familiar with this, perhaps it is not something you have done in the past, something your family did not do when you were growing up. That's ok, now is a good time to start. It is a good thing to develop together and it only takes one of you to get it started.

The spousal relationship is the perfect fertile ground for charity and generosity. This makes things possible that were not before. In this relationship we discover things inside of us we did not know existed, just waiting to come to life.

Sharing and helping others is a remarkable thing—you will feel great when you enrich the lives of others. It's a remarkable experience, both in the moment of sharing and over time. It is something you will always remember and something you will never regret.

Who looks back over their life and feels they should not have shared, or shared too much? Nobody of course.

People have a strong sense of right and wrong. However, sometimes we become distracted by the many things that demand our time and attention in our increasingly crazy world.

But when we see something fundamentally good, it reminds us of what might be lying inside of us and waiting for the right time to come alive.

Waiting to be awakened by something small. Witnessing an act of charity, an act of kindness, an act of sharing can trigger others to share in kind. This is a remarkable legacy to stimulate and nurture.

Be open and be humble with your acts of charity and you will likely see others take up the same commitment.

The act of sharing has a profound impact on those around us and even those we don't know.

It could be a complete stranger that we influence. It could be anybody.

Should your marriage be blessed with children, your acts of charity will change how your children view many things going forward through their lives. Your friends will know, your extended family will know and those you come in contact with will know that you are sharing with others, helping others. For children, something good can lie waiting patiently inside of them and come alive when triggered many years later.

For some, likely for most, they will decide they want to be part of this compelling thing and will begin sharing as well. This is something that pulls us in, a wonderful force of good that spreads.

Sharing is contagious.

Sharing is something other people want to be part of. There is no better place to start than in a marriage.

When we have the opportunity to help others that are struggling with homelessness or lack of basic necessities, don't assume they will benefit more than we do from our work. When we take the time to spend time with and talk with those in need of help, we can learn a great deal if we just listen.

Saint Vincent de Paul said 'The poor have much to teach you. You have much to learn from them.'

This is yet another reminder there is always more to people than we might assume and we should never be too impressed with ourselves or our station. Humility helps to protect us.

The combination of you and your spouse sharing is powerful, much more powerful than a single person. You will discover that sharing and charity can be an engine of joy and enrichment in your marriage.

When we do something together, it creates a strong sense of unity, a strong sense of good, a strong sense of trust. It is a reminder of the wonderful power of 'we' in our marriage and what you and your spouse are capable of together.

A day with sharing, of helping others, is a day more complete.

It creates a remarkable sense of accomplishment that is bound-less really in the good that it creates in our lives.

Praise

TRUTH #13

We all love to be told we've done well by the people we care about.

We even love to be told we did something good by people we don't know. We just love to hear good stuff—it is wired into all of us.

This is an important idea to take forward in our marriage. Praise your spouse for the little things and the big things they do for us. Be grateful every day.

Never miss an opportunity to say 'thank you', or 'I really appreciate that', or 'that made me feel good'. We simply can't say thanks enough. When we recognize a good deed and are grateful, those good things and those good deeds are much more likely to happen again. This is a wonderful and powerful cycle.

Work hard at being thankful and grateful.

Don't let the passing of years lessen your commitment to both say-ing thanks for a kind and thoughtful act by your spouse, or in rec-ognizing something your spouse has done that is good, something that helped someone else, something you appreciate.

These things can fade in a marriage over time, so don't let it fade in yours.

Maybe your spouse did something nice for a friend of yours, be sure to recognize it. Perhaps your spouse helped your mom or dad, be sure to tell them how much you appreciate that.

That is a big one.

It could be your spouse met an important deadline or got a pro-motion at work, it's important to say you are proud of them—work should be kept in the proper perspective but the work done by your spouse does help to provide for you and the family so it's important.

I can't think of anything that made me feel better than the times Julie has told me she is proud of me. It's an amazing thing to hear this from your spouse. Just amazing.

Commit to making this a normal part of your day—giving thanks to your spouse for the little things they do during the day. A sin-cere thank you is a very powerful thing.

My wife does not like to speak in public—like many adults, the thought of this makes her very nervous. But, Julie was asked to give a talk at our church, to about 1,000 people no-less, and she agreed to do it because she felt it was the right thing to do (of course). She came up with a plan and worked super hard to be ready for that day, and she was just awesome! She absolutely nailed it. I was so proud of her, and the whole family made a big deal out of it and we had a nice celebration dinner.

My Julie was a star that day. We all knew it was very important to her and the whole family told her how great she was about a hundred times that night and the next day. She was beaming for about a week and she had overcame one of her biggest life fears, and that took strength and courage. She is a very tough lady. Now, she knows she can do it and has put that fear behind her forever. I was so happy to be part of it.

You likely have your own stories, and there will be many more of these in the future.

When they happen, seize the moment with praise and appreciation.

You will know when something is important to your spouse and when they do well, tell them they did a great job, and tell them again. Then tell them again.

Also, if your spouse gives something their best and the outcome is not what they had hoped, tell them it is ok. We are proud of them for giving their best effort. This is just as important as the big success. So much in life is about trying and giving our best.

There is no higher form of praise than what comes from your spouse, the person you respect and love most of all.

Never underestimate the power of the simple words of praise.

And yes, they are part of the cycle of good stuff that is likely to come back to you when you do something great too.

Remember how good that feels.

Celebration

TRUTH #14

We will have good days and there will be bad days.

Likely, many more of the good than the bad.

Life holds great joys, a few miracles, and some tough challenges. This is the case for all of us. In marriage, we face the good times and the tough times together, as a team, and this builds our special bond, a unique bond that can only come from the test of good and bad.

The joys of the good and the tests of the bad galvanize our marriage.

Good times are pretty easy, that's no surprise. But we learn a lot about ourselves, about our spouse, and about our marriage when the tough times come.

When we do conquer challenges, when we do hit an important mile-stone, when we do clear one of life's hurdles, it's time to celebrate!

Big celebrations and small celebrations—they are all important. Take celebration seriously, make it something you are good at. A big part of the fun celebrations bring us is looking forward to them. Savoring them. Take your time and plan ahead.

Make it a lifestyle to celebrate success, savor the little victories that life creates for us. It can be virtually anything—there are no rules here but the ones you make and when in doubt, celebrate!

Celebrate birthdays. They are a big deal.

Celebrate moving into your first home. This is a very big deal.

Celebrate moving to a new flat or apartment. It's an important step.

Celebrate a promotion at work. They help us provide for our family.

Celebrate a good doctor appointment. Sure, this is a big relief.

Celebrate returning from a long trip if you and your spouse were separated. These are not easy.

Celebrate a good performance review at work. They help to build our careers.

If you have children, they create many more reasons to celebrate.

A good report card should be celebrated. School is important.

Learning to ride a bike or drive a car should be celebrated. A milestone we will always remember.

Got your drivers license? That is a big day and life changes forever.

A successful recital should be celebrated. A proud moment for parents.

A big win in sports should be celebrated. These are a lot of fun.

Celebrate the birthday of your spouse. This is a important day and they should feel special. Take the time to give thoughtful presents, and a nice dinner with a favorite dessert.

This is celebrating the passing of our time together and everybody loves some attention on their birthday. We never outgrow that.

And of course, celebrate your wedding anniversary, it is a very, very big deal and should be a unique celebration all it's own.

The anniversary should be a level above the other days because your marriage is above the other things.

Maybe celebrate by going back to where you had your first date. This is not a time to go cheap or to cut corners. Do something you normally don't do to keep the wedding anniversary celebration in a category all it's own.

We don't need to make these celebrations too elaborate or too expensive because that misses the point. We don't want to create a reason to do them less.

No, the whole point is recognition, of savoring the moment.

Taking the time to enjoy one of the joys life brings us. Some of the best celebrations can be simple. Cooking dinner for your spouse. Bringing your spouse a favorite dessert and sharing it after a meal. A special card. Surprise them with flowers, or a small gift.

It can be anything, and you will know what works best.

Make celebration part of your lifestyle. Make celebration fundamental to your marriage because it says so much. A celebration is recognition, thoughtfulness, caring, joy and fun all mixed into one amazing package.

How good is that?

Have you missed something that should have been celebrated? Well, it's not too late, have that celebration now and don't miss the next one.

Make it a fun thing and celebrate the one that got away.

You will never regret a celebration, they are just too much fun and just too naturally good.

We will only regret the celebrations we let slip away so let's not let that happen.

Chores

TRUTH #15

*Y*es, we need to consider chores for a few minutes. Not sexy but important nonetheless.

They can be no fun but they are part of every household and every marriage. Work has to be done to keep the home running. Whether you share a small apartment or a bigger home, or a working farm there are chores to be done every day.

Where there are chores there needs to be a plan. Because without a plan there will be friction between you and your spouse and friction can grow into a bigger problem. We need to push friction out of our life where we can.

First, it's good to understand a couple of things including what you and your spouse are good at or uniquely able to do, and then what your spouse prefers to do.

The second part of that is important because we are going to make a sacrifice here.

I strongly recommend allowing your spouse to pick first when it comes to the chore list. It's a small thing, but small things make a difference over time. Yes, I know, that is not what we really want to do, but let's give them this one. It really helps to make everybody happy.

Of course there will be things that you must do and that is fine. But for the stuff that both of you are capable of doing, give your spouse the wonderful gift of allowing them to pick first from the chore list. Give them the first draft pick.

Make it fun—you can even use this for a little leverage later in the day. This could be another case of a negotiation in the making. After all, we should never miss an opportunity to negotiate an outcome that both you and your spouse feel good about.

It's a good practice to tackle chores together. Try to do them at the same time when you can.

Saturday mornings for example are a time when many of us are getting things done around the house. Together is always good. I recommend doing chores in the morning when possible, when you are fresh and the day is new, do them together and then have a little reward when you are done.

Something to look forward to is always a good thing, like sharing a coffee or tea, or having breakfast after you get all or part of your list done. Start with the hard stuff first and just get it done. That feels really good and then everything is a little easier.

If you finish before your spouse does, then go and help them finish their work. Don't just sit down and wait. Maybe that's obvious but it bears mentioning because you just never know.

Be gracious in giving a helping hand. You are not done until both of you are done.

Try to keep a good attitude because it makes a big difference. This is one of those times when it's easy to slide into a bad mood and then that will affect your spouse and then your day starts to get worse. This is fully under our control.

All of this can be prevented, so just make up your mind to make the best of chores, get them knocked out as quickly as you can, together, and then get on with having a great day.

If you have kids, make sure they're helping out. Give them a list of what they can do. Or make a master list and let them pick from the list and encourage them to get their chores done together with you and your spouse. Make it a family activity and it will go even faster. Don't let people get grumpy and remember that you can set the example. Yes, I know it's not easy but you can do it.

Speaking of examples, you can set an example for your spouse. If you are doing your chores with a bad attitude and getting worse by the minute, then what is going to happen with your spouse? Exactly. I've been guilty of this more than a few times.

However, if you have a good attitude and keep it light and fun, then that is exactly how your spouse is going to be. Simple, but it does make a difference so let's not let getting a few things done around the house drag us down.

As with so many daily things, we can turn a potentially painful thing into something fun. Or, at least bearable.

Money

TRUTH #16

*M*oney might cause more arguments and stress in a marriage than anything else.

Money can be complicated and it can be very emotional. This doesn't make it any easier.

And, money issues change over time as we go through the many stages of life. There will be times when the money is there, and times when it's not.

There will be times when things are tight and you are just not sure how the bills will get paid. That is a very stressful time, a tremendous weight on your marriage and a time that comes for most of us.

But like most things in marriage, it's best to tackle money issues as a team.

Have a plan that allows you to work together through those tough times and to enjoy the good times when they come.

It's even better to have both a short-term plan and a long-term plan. The short-term plan can be how you are going to pay the bills now and meet other commitments in the next year and then a long-term plan that looks at milestones like retirement. These plans can be very simple and should be developed together so then you and your spouse can implement the plan together every day.

This helps to avoid misunderstandings, to avoid confusion and keeps you and your spouse on the same page.

Of course, the goals of your plan and how you manage money every day are different for everybody so there is no single and simple formula for managing money in your marriage. Unless you are one of the very, very few, money will be an issue from time to time so we need to be keenly aware of the challenges this can create in a marriage.

It's a big deal in our day to day lives.

So, let's go over a few basics that might help.

First, it helps to have a working monthly budget that you and your spouse have developed together with lots of discussion, and that both of you understand well.

This is not a budget of optimism or of worst case, but one that is your best estimate of reality. Make sure all your monthly and regularly occurring bills including things like rent/mortgage, groceries, meals out, entertainment, vacations, utilities, cell phones, gasoline, school tuition, car maintenance, and savings are included.

The budget should also include some amount for discretionary spending. Things like seasonal clothing purchases, birthday and holiday gifts, special purchases, and the like should be included. Do your best to build a full stack of expenses that accurately capture monthly and yearly spending. Then, we lay in our income, whether one spouse is working or both of you work you should have a pretty good idea of the income side and then we reconcile this against the expenses.

This is not a book on budgets as much fun as that would be, so we will leave the subject there, but again the key is to develop the monthly budget together so that when things get tight you and your spouse are in synch on where the money is going and can then work through any issues that arise.

They key here is not that managing our money will be easy, it isn't, but that you and your spouse do it together and have a shared voice.

You might have picked up that I'm not a fan of the model where you or your spouse know everything about the budget, manage the money, pays the bills, and the other spouse knows nothing about it and the numbers.

Now having said that, some couples are able to do this single-spouse-budget-thing and they manage to make it work so this is certainly not a fatal blow in a marriage. If that model works for your marriage, that is great. But for most marriages the challenges come when things get tight and if you are not managing the money issues together you or your spouse will not know what's going on, will not understand the number, will not be invested in the plan, and so it then gets much harder to solve the challenges together and to both be engaged in the process and what comes next.

The bottom line is that we need to keep money is perspective,

it is simply a necessary thing, a reality of life and a reality of our marriage and we can't let it consume us.

Sometimes we need to take a step back and realize that any challenges we are facing with money will be manageable over time and the happiness of our marriage can't and won't be dragged down by money. The money is the money and we have managed through anything together and this is just another thing.

When that time does come and when it seems so overwhelming, you or your spouse needs to take a step back and remind both of you,

'we will get through this together, and it will be ok—we have each other and that is all that matters.'

Everything else is secondary. It won't make it easy, but it helps to keep things in perspective, in balance.

This holds true for the other issues that we can feel are so big in a marriage. All that really matters, is the two of you loving each other, supporting each other, and working together through anything that life brings our way.

Family, money, jobs, illness and anything else. It doesn't matter.

What matters most is our marriage, happy and together through better or worse, always. That's it.

Family

Truth #17

*W*hen we marry, when we have taken those sacred vows and go back down the aisle together, we become part of a bigger family. It might be much bigger, or only a little bigger but we take on the family of our spouse and that family will be part of our journey in marriage for the rest of our lives.

This will be important to our spouse and so it becomes important to us.

This is one of those issues that is a fundamental part of our day-to-day marriage but one we might not think a lot about before we are married.

Yes, we of course know that our spouse has family, parents, brothers or sisters perhaps, but we don't naturally think about the day-to-day life with this extended family. What does it mean for holidays?

What does it mean for vacations? Will there be regular family get-togethers? To what degree will your spouse's family be involved in your daily lives, in particular if they live locally?

Much has been said about mothers-in-law and fathers-in-law, but you might be surprised to discover these are really great people. I know that mine are.

After all, they did raise your spouse, the person you love so much. There is something to be said for that. They did a lot right.

From the very beginning, try to put your spouse's parents at ease. Let them know they are important to you and you want them to be part of your life.

You can figure out the details later but understand they will be a little nervous and a little worried about how things will change now that their little girl/boy is married. Don't let these concerns linger, and just talk about it right up front.

Be kind and be thoughtful, and everybody will be happier.

It is only natural that you won't always agree with or get along with your spouse's family. That's ok. Remember—you don't always get along with your own parents, your own siblings, all the time either.

The family of your spouse should be treated with the same patience and consideration as your own family. In all things, and every day.

In particular, the parents of your spouse. Give them your respect, give them your best. It is important to your spouse and it is important to your marriage. Don't let this create a source of friction in your home. As with a few of our earlier topics, we want to push friction out of our marriage every chance we get. This is so preventable, and completely under your control.

In some marriages, there seems to be a standard for our own family and then a different standard for how we act and think towards the family of our spouse. Common yes, natural, perhaps a bit, but ultimately this is not a good thing. This is not going to support a happy marriage over time and we need to be careful to not settle into this behavior.

When dealing with the parents of your spouse, think for a moment about what you would do with your own parents.

When thinking about the siblings of our spouse, take a minute to reflect on what you would do with your own brother or sister. This changes things. It is also something your spouse will appreciate and a simple and small shift in mindset can prevent lots of potential problems in the future. You will live the rest of your life with your spouse's family so commit to giving them the consideration and respect worthy of your spouse.

Build a solid foundation for the future.

Like other things, when we are committed to treating the family of our spouse with the same patience and consideration as our own family, everything gets better, everything gets a bit easier. Even better, our spouse will want to return the favor. This is a wonderful thing—both you and your spouse treating your respective families really well. It's good for everybody.

Happy to have them included, treating them with love and patience.

You might note that I've used the word 'patience' here several times.

That is no accident my friends and in particular how it relates to the parents of your spouse.

How you treat the mom and dad of your spouse says a lot about You. Not them, but You. Don't forget that.

These people have nurtured, raised, loved and shaped the love of your life. As such, there is a lot of goodness in them. Never forget this and it should become the basis for your respect and patience, especially given they are likely aging, in retirement at some point, perhaps challenged with health issues and the other natural bumps that occur when we enter our later years.

Be a source of comfort and a helping hand for both your parents and the parents of your spouse as they age.

This is the right thing to do, this is the essence of a family.

Faithfulness

TRUTH #18

No discussion on marriage would be complete without spending some time on faithfulness.

Although not an easy or comfortable topic it just can't be ignored. It is so central, so fundamental to the vows we took on the day of our wedding and the daily commitment we make to our spouse.

We started the book with a discussion of these vows and the promise that is at the heart of our marriage. At the heart of our promise is our pledge to be faithful.

I promise to be true to you in good times and in bad...

This promise is so simple and so powerful—and it says so much. It says that we will stay together when life is hard and not just when life is good, and that we will love our spouse as no other person and we will never stray.

No matter what happens, no matter what life throws at us we will face it together, as long as we are alive. Only death can take us from each other and from our vows.

Not an easy promise of course but this is the foundation on which a happy and lasting marriage must be built.

There is another side to faithfulness that we need to address—and be very clear there is simply no greater and deeper poison in a marriage than that of infidelity. This is a terrible and selfish act that can destroy everything we work so hard for. It shatters our promise.

You must simply commit, with every ounce of your will, to be faithful to your spouse every day and every year of your marriage.

There will be times when we are frustrated with our spouse, when we are working through challenging times, when we don't feel as close as we would like. We might sink to a dark place for a while.

This is not easy, but it happens to many marriages. When these challenging times come and they do come, and we experience the flood of emotions that come with them, the one thing we absolutely must do is remain faithful.

We don't seek comfort, or a distraction, or some fleeting excitement with another person. This never makes things better. Never.

Cheating is just not an option. No matter what.

Leaving is not an option.

We stay together. No matter what.

We keep the promise we made on our wedding day. When things get hard, this is a time to be strong and our spouse is worth it. And in every case we will be glad that we were strong and faithful later when the challenge is behind us.

Any frustration or disappointment with our spouse will pass and then we are left with the satisfaction of keeping our promise, of keeping our vows. We never regret being strong for our spouse.

Tomorrow is a new day with new hope.

Understand that in most cases the final act of adultery was enabled through many small steps that led up to that moment.

It is important, really more than important, it is absolutely critical that we are aware of the actions we take every day and how these actions and our words might be interpreted by others. We can't allow ourselves to take the little steps, to walk the path that can lead to an affair. If you become aware this is happening, just stop. Pay attention.

The greatest single thing we can do to prevent an act of being unfaithful is to simply avoid putting ourselves in a position that could lead directly to the final act.

Even more, we must avoid accepting any signals of interest from other men or women. At the same time, take great care to not send our own signals. Even small things matter and we just can't do that stuff.

A simple thing, but very important and an awareness we need to have every day.

We can be strong because our spouse is worth it.

In today's world, with distractions including social media, mobile phones and easy access to the internet and all it brings—the greatest evil of which is likely pornography, we need to steer clear of these things that weaken our bond and our devotion to our spouse.

Pornography is another form of infidelity.

It has been proven that pornography creates a reaction in our brain that is similar to, or even greater than that of the strongest drug.

This is part of what has created the explosion of the pornography industry today.

Don't let this become part of your life, just don't start. If you have already started this, make a commitment to stop now.

If you are struggling with pornography, a resource that can help is *www.reclaimsexualhealth.com*. Note that I have no relationship with and receive no compensation from this organization.

An addiction to pornography cripples, or completely destroys our ability to love our spouse completely. It is hard to overstate the importance of quitting pornography if you do it today, or never starting this addiction if you don't do it today.

Looking at pornography objectifies your spouse—it fundamentally changes how you see your spouse and it begins to destroy the closeness, love and intimacy that is so important in a healthy marriage.

Be strong. Your spouse is worth it. Battle this evil. Your spouse is worth it.

Maybe this was something you did before your marriage—be honest with yourself about this being a big problem. Then, commit to stopping today.

If you have never looked at pornography, that is great. But, it is important to understand how damaging this can be in a marriage so make a commitment now to never start. It helps to be aware of what is at stake here.

A couple of final thoughts on faithfulness and these are tough ones that I urge you to think about, to pray about, and to consider carefully as you might not agree initially with what I recommend.

First, if you have had an affair, you are likely experiencing the mix of powerful emotions that happen in the days and weeks and years following.

But this terrible thing is now done, you can't go back, but you must promise to never doing it again. Absolutely, never again. No matter what.

The future is something that is fully under your control and it's important you are stronger, more aware and much more careful in the future. It just can't happen again. Give your spouse the gift of remaining faithful for the rest of your lives together. Learn from this terrible mistake and commit to being stronger. It's just not worth it and you surely know that now.

Pray for strength, and you will get the help you need.

Second, if your spouse has had an affair, you must forgive them.

Yes, the anger and betrayal are overwhelming and forgiving might seem impossible. But, as hard as it will be, you must forgive them and save the future of your marriage. Heal slowly together and leave this terrible thing behind you.

As hard as it might be to understand now, this painful thing that has come between you is much smaller than the infinitely greater and lasting pain and impact to so many lives caused by a marriage failing.

I appreciate this is a very difficult decision to make and feels like your heart is being ripped from your chest—but this is the right decision. Forgive and then take the time together to rebuild the trust. This healing won't happen quickly, and likely will take years but as the healing and forgiveness happens, you have saved a marriage, something that is worth saving more so than anything else in our lives is worth saving.

The effects of a failed marriage last for years and often for generations. Yes, for generations. Think about that.

The waves of pain extend far and wide. This is not an easy thing to come to peace with, and it might be the most difficult thing you have ever done, but we will go to extreme lengths in order to save the most important thing we will ever do.

If you have children, it is even more important to do whatever it takes to save your marriage.

The day you make this incredibly difficult decision, is the

beginning of the healing. It will be slow, but you will get through this and you will have done an incredible good for your family.

Rebuilding the trust will not be easy. But, it can be done and saving your marriage is a miracle and a gift to your spouse that you might feel they are not worthy of, but they are.

You will understand that later.

Let's close this discussion by going back to the idea of prevention, of remaining faithful to your spouse every day and avoiding the pain of infidelity and all it brings.

Keep your promise, no matter what.

Poisons

TRUTH #19

*S*ome thoughts and actions that are somewhat harmless or meaningless in daily life outside a marriage, can be poisons within a marriage.

Big and small alike, we need to avoid these poisons that weaken our marriage, erode what is so special about the bond we have with our spouse.

Always respect your spouse. Always. Give them the benefit of the doubt. Always. They deserve it.

If we have any issues that need to be discussed do it as soon as possible and always hear what your spouse has to say first. Never air issues for the first time when with family or friends. It's not the time unless the issue has first been discussed with your spouse and you and your spouse have agreed to get input from family or friends. At the right time, in the right way this can be a good thing.

Parents for example can be a great sounding board when needed.

Be careful with sarcasm.

For some families this is a normal way of joking but many people are not comfortable with sarcasm so just be careful and it might be best to leave this behind. You will know what your spouse is and is not comfortable with. It should be mentioned there is a big difference between a little light-hearted sarcasm and sarcasm with a streak of meanness running through it. Sarcasm with an edge. A big difference.

This shows up in couples that are struggling with their marriage and they might not even be aware of it. So please be careful.

Treat each other kindly. Genuine kindness says so much. Kindness is borne of trust, respect and love.

It is not unusual to have spouses talk to each other and act toward one another with something that is a lot less than complete respect. This is a bad habit of sorts that builds over time. Just a little bit at a time and then the day comes when what is said between these spouses is hard to listen to. It seems like every comment is an accusation or underlined with disappointment. You might know a couple like this.

Make a commitment now to not allow this to happen.

Don't be sloppy with respect and kindness and don't allow this to creep into your marriage. Always be vigilant—they deserve it and you promised it on the day of your wedding.

Any friends or even strangers that spend time with you and your spouse should be left with the impression that you are very much a couple in love. A few months after your wedding, or 5 years, or 50 years later. This never changes.

Good days and tough days will come and go as the natural rhythm of life, but this cannot break down who we are.

If anything, this amazing journey of life and marriage should bring us closer together. Have the mindset that alone we are weak, but together we are strong and can get through anything.

There will be times when we are tired, when we are frustrated and when we are not happy with something our spouse has done or said. Remember, this is natural and is not something that can impact our respect and love.

A lack of communication is another poison to guard against. Protect against silence, this is a void that can grow. Talk about everything, big and small. Share everything.

Don't let silence become the norm. Don't let silence grow as the years pass and fill your home.

Always share your feelings openly with your spouse, tell them what you like and don't like. Tell them what makes you happy and what makes you sad. Nothing is off limits—nothing is too big or too small.

Complete honesty is an amazing gift in a marriage and something you and your spouse are in complete control of. This is the perfect place for perfect honesty to grow.

It brings you closer together, it builds the respect that is so vital to a marriage. Share the highlights of your day. They will love to hear it and will want to share the same with you.

My family plays a little game around the dinner table called 'High-Low'. We each take turns sharing our highs and lows from the day. This is always good for a few laughs and a few surprises. Sharing is good, openness is good. Talking about the day is good. This is fun stuff and healthy. It keeps us close.

Happy couples will in almost every case be committed to communicating and sharing. This might not be natural in the beginning but with commitment it will become more comfortable over time. Work at it. Think of this as you and your spouse training and encouraging each other to be more honest and more open.

Build another good habit.

Good will conquer bad if only we give it a little help.

Dating

TRUTH #20

*T*hink back for a moment to when you and your spouse first met. How did you feel? What was the first thing you noticed about them? Maybe their smile. Maybe they made you laugh. Maybe they just had something special and you weren't sure yet exactly what it was. But it was there.

Maybe it was love at first sight, or maybe you were friends first and then it became something more later.

We all have our story.

You might have had a short whirlwind courtship or you might have been together for a long time before getting married. Your feelings might have grown slowly or come all at once is a dizzying rush.

It could have been anything, and it is special for all of us. We love thinking about the beginning.

Regardless of the unique path that brought us together in marriage, there was a time when you and your spouse dated. This is when we fell in love and discovered all the little things that make our spouse one of a kind.

They were made for us and there is nobody else like them.

Well, it's important that we never stop dating.

These dates can be anything that works for you and for your schedule. These dates can be dinners on the weekend with just the two of you. They can be lunches during the week.

Or, they can be breakfast on the weekend which is what I enjoy with Julie. The house is quiet early in the morning and we get away for a little while to have breakfast and slow things down. Just the two of us.

Your dates are a good time to share and to laugh. To reflect on the great things that happened in the last week, and to talk about upcoming decisions or anything else that needs attention.

It doesn't matter what kind of date works, make time to get away.

Find a dating plan that is comfortable, something that will work over time and at a time and in a way that you both feel good about and enjoy. Remember, this could be anything, there are no rules.

Then, don't let anything stand in the way of your little excursions.

Life will get busy, it will get crazy at times, work will be stressful, and that is all to be expected.

Regardless of what is swirling around you in daily life, make time for your dates. These are priceless.

This time together is a reminder of why you love your spouse so much, why they are special, a reminder of all the things you discovered about them when you first met and when you first fell in love.

Sometimes life can be overwhelming and we are just trying to survive. Remember, we should do this together and not apart. Share how you are feeling on one of your dates and ask for help. Your spouse will appreciate the honesty, after all they know you better than anybody and are likely to be in the best position to help.

Share something good that happened to you this week. Share something that upset you. Tell your spouse about something that reminded you of them. These little things are important.

We all love hearing about these little things that happen in life, we just need to take the time to share. It only takes a minute or two and it forms a habit that will stick with us. This is yet another little thing that weaves the bond that is so vital to marriage. It is just as much about the little stuff as it is about the big stuff. This is the tapestry of marriage.

Yes, the big stuff does matter but day in and day out, we spend more of our time on the little things, the little challenges that are placed in our path, and the nurturing we do to keep our marriage strong.

In the absence of our dates and in the absence of the other twenty-five truths, we can drift apart. This does not happen overnight, it happens a little bit at a time. Then, we wake up one day and realize that something is missing in our marriage and it is not what we want it to be.

Not what it was at one time.

But, with our dates we stay close, we stay connected and tied together and don't allow ourselves to drift.

Our little dates are a big anchor.

We stay united in facing everything that comes our way and in enjoying and celebrating all the wonderful things our marriage can create.

There is a fine line here and it only requires a bit of our attention to stay on the side of happy and healthy and together.

Children

TRUTH #21

Not all marriages will include children—this is not fully under our control and we are all traveling our own path.

But, if your marriage has been blessed with children it is important to recognize a few important things this brings. Julie and I have six amazing kids and the day the first child arrived, everything changed forever. It does for all of us.

New challenges are created, and new joys are now possible.

Suddenly we see everything differently, we change our view of the hours in the day and what the night brings, our schedule becomes completely different, our life goals change, how we eat changes, how we plan the budget, our sleep schedule, our friends will change too and this is just the beginning.

We even change how we dress—yes, we could be spit up on at any time and we can really use more pockets now.

It can be said that children will likely bring us some of the hardest moments and decisions of our lives while at the same time bringing us some of the greatest joys of our life.

Kids are uniquely capable of this.

Children in a marriage also causes us to think about and then create a new balance of time. Children depend on us for everything in the beginning, and over time these needs change but they never completely go away until that day your child moves out of your home, beginning a new life on their own. Even then, they might come back for a while. You just never know and that is yet another crazy thing a kid brings to your life—an element of unpredictability.

Oh goodness, is that ever true. Don't ever think for a minute that you know what's coming next with your kids.

As we try to find this new balance of our time and energy it is a good time to remember where we started—nothing is more important than our marriage.

Yes, our children need us and demand so much of our time, but these needs can't be taken to the degree that our marriage begins to suffer. Our marriage comes first. In the beginning, and always.

This is an important point that might surprise you—sometimes the kids will need to wait while we spend some time with, while we focus on, and while we give our spouse our full attention and affection.

The kids can't and should not always come first. Even with children, our marriage is the foundation.

It's ok, the kids will be fine. Kids are remarkably resilient and they will be fine. Of course, we are not talking about hardship here, we are simply talking about you and your spouse planning a dinner out together while a trusted sitter, cousin, or friend watches the kids.

Julie and I are big believers in doing virtually everything as a family. This is when we create priceless memories and this brings the family closer together. But it is important, even more than important, it is vital that we find time to focus on each other, to get away for our little dates. Be creative, it's not that hard really. These are little getaways, an hour or two at a time.

On vacations, take the kids. These are experiences everybody will remember and treasure in the future. Yes, the kids make vacations a little more complicated and a little more expensive, but don't underestimate the closeness and happiness this brings the family. Some of our best memories are on family vacations when the kids did something amazing, or did something completely unexpected.

Remember that your children need a happy and healthy marriage in which to thrive, in which to become the best people they can be.

So we must continue to focus on our marriage for the sake of our marriage of course, but also for the sake of our children.

As parents, we are role modeling for our children every minute of every day and a marriage that is happy, a marriage where the father respects the mother and the mother respects the father means so much to children and ultimately does so much to determine how our children will think and act in their own marriages some day.

This is a remarkable gift we can give our children—loving our husband or wife unconditionally and giving them our best every day. This creates a loving, patient, faithful and hopeful household.

Children will then give so much back to their parents and to the household. Really, beyond the home children bring so much to our world.

In his famous Letter to Children in December of 1994, Pope John Paul II said '… It is true that a child represents the joy not only of its parents… but the whole of society'.

Children bring an innocence and purity of spirit that is so much of what is needed in our marriage and in our culture—a culture that is so often lacking these qualities that must be nurtured if we are to have the future we hope to preserve for future generations. Only from marriage can this be.

Work

TRUTH #22

Our jobs and our work have a natural place in our lives.

Yes, work is important because it does provide the income we need for the basics of life. But this does change the day we are married. Not that work goes away, but that it yields to our marriage and all our priorities are adjusted. The reality is that work is the #1 priority for many single people before they are married.

But, all our priorities will be reassessed both through our own eyes and through the shared eyes of our marriage. What is important to our spouse becomes important to us.

Regardless of the new priority rank we will create with our spouse, our marriage now takes top priority.

Make no mistake, for most people work will continue to be a large time commitment and to simply have a necessary place in our lives. But when the time comes and work begins to assert greater pressure on our marriage it is time to recalibrate things.

This is a time to bring our priorities back into balance and to remember where we started—that our marriage takes priority over all other things. No exceptions.

It is not unusual for this realignment of our lives to happen from time to time. It is not only natural, it is healthy. This realignment can be driven by our work of course, but also by children, by aging parents, by our retirement plans and much more.

So much demands our time, so much creates pressure and so much occupies our thinking. However, while this blurring might happen temporarily, there can be no questioning what priority remains #1 and will always be number one when the time for rebalancing our life and how we spend our time comes.

It is our marriage and only our marriage. Then, look to love and prayer to nurture our marriage more than everything else.

This could simply be the three things that give us all we need to know when we are in need of simplicity. Put love, prayer and marriage at the center of our daily lives, and we can't go too far off track.

It can be said that nothing can become great, nothing can become strong without minding the fundamentals. Well, that is our marriage and with that we always go back to love and prayer.

It is also perhaps true that one of the greatest risks to our marriage is a demanding job.

I do appreciate that virtually every marriage is different as there are countless variables in the union of two.

But a demanding job is nearly boundless in it's demand for our mind and energy and time and so it takes away so much of what we have to give.

This is why it is so important to bring our job back into balance with our marriage. This can be a very simple thing. For example, if we find ourselves working later and later, it is time to set a 'curfew' of sorts, a time to go home and be with our spouse. That extra hour at the office each day just isn't worth it.

It could mean turning off the laptop, or the phone or email for a couple of quiet hours in the evening so we can give time back to our spouse.

It could be anything, so discuss this with your spouse and create a plan to give some time back to your marriage and take precious time and heart back from a greedy job.

It's also a good practice to share what's happening in our job with our spouse. Tell them everything. Tell them about the good stuff and tell them about the bad stuff.

Share with your spouse when something good happens at work, when you get recognized or when you complete an important project. If you closed a new deal, or helped an existing customer, tell your spouse about it. Be sure to tell them when you are struggling or frustrated with your boss or anything else that can make you discouraged.

This sharing and openness is important because your spouse will then understand when you seem a little down, when something is on your mind.

With that understanding, your spouse can help you work through it and can likely give you some good advice. But, they can only help if you let them know what's happening at work.

We close this discussion with going back to the idea of calibrating your time now and then and recognizing you might need to take some time back from the demands of your job and invest the time with your spouse, more time with the family. Always be aware of this balance. Jobs are greedy, jobs can carry us away. And the more responsibility we earn at work, the more success we have, the more demanding our jobs become. But they are not the most important thing.

The decision to give more time back to our marriage and back to our family is one decision we will never regret.

Trust

TRUTH #23

It is not possible to build a lasting marriage without trust.

Trust is so fundamental to any lasting relationship, and so to our marriage.

The journey of trust is one of many small steps, not of a single leap.

Our words can encourage trust but trust can only be shaped and galvanized through our actions. It is always best to both verbalize and to then act. But if only one is possible, our actions mean so much more that our words ever could.

There are no shortcuts to trust. Do what you say you will do. Simple but not easy.

But being aware of this relationship, the relationship between our words and actions, and of our responsibility as a spouse does make us aware and with that awareness it does get a little easier to build trust.

Be mindful of this connection—our actions every day, the little and big things that we do, they are what bring trust. Then, with trust anything is possible in our marriage. No test is too big, to challenge is too difficult. And trust is not just about meeting challenges. Trust is much more. Trust brings us closer together and allows us to more completely share all the little and wonderful joys marriage can bring. Accomplishing a life goal, a big promotion at work, a special vacation, the birth of a child, celebrating an anniversary, or virtually anything that is important to us becomes more meaningful with trust.

It is a fundamental truth that where there is trust, you will surely find a strong marriage and where trust is missing, you will surely find a marriage struggling.

Every day we have the opportunity to build trust and we should recognize this as an important part of the journey with our spouse. This is a good thing so see it as an opportunity. When we make a commitment we should do so thoughtfully and knowing we will keep it. No matter what. We are good to our word and we take it very seriously. This builds trust.

Saint Camillus, a remarkably strong and compassionate man and founder of the original Red Cross organization said 'Commitment is doing what you said you would do, after the feeling you said it in has passed'.

If there has been anybody in our lives worthy of building trust with and for, it is surely our spouse. Always take care in understanding that what we are about to say and what we are about to do, will build or erode the trust just a little bit more.

This calls us to explore yet *another dimension to the spousal relationship* and that is the commitment and trust we share. This trust with our spouse is unlike any other, forged by vows and the tests that our world and our journey brings us. Being tested, being challenged galvanizes trust.

Trust is closely linked to honesty. Honesty naturally builds trust and a lack of honesty will weaken our ability to build trust. There is so much good that comes from complete honesty, only one of these being trust.

Like many other things in marriage, it is simple but anything but easy.

Do what we say we will do, and don't do what we say we won't do.

Follow this formula every day.

If we really know we can't do something, then don't say we will. Yes, we really want to say what our spouse wants to hear, that is natural. But if we know it won't happen, then don't say it will. Conversely, if we know we are going to do something that won't make our spouse happy, then best to be upfront.

This is not good news, but it does build the trust.

It's important to understand that sometimes there will be bad news and it's best to just come right out with it.

Bad news does not get better with time.

We wish it did, but that is just not the case. Delivering bad news when it is necessary and not trying to stall or hide it, is another behavior that builds the trust in our marriage.

Then, when we set this standard together, it fosters the total honesty and openness that we find in the very best marriages, and the very best relationships as well.

Take the good and the bad head on. This is trust in action.

Goals

TRUTH #24

When we come together in marriage, things that did not matter as much before now become a very big deal and move to the center of our marriage and our daily lives.

One such thing are our short-term and long-term goals. Life goals if you will.

Not always something we discussed when dating, these become very important now that we are traveling this journey with our spouse.

We need to be pointed in the same direction. We need to be working together to make these goals a reality. We need to be supportive of one another.

This requires some honesty, communication and patience. Maybe our goals are very similar, and maybe they are very different. Either is ok because all that matters is that we begin to come together, to find some common ground because we are much stronger and much more productive as a team. Yes, and happier too.

These goals can include things like financial matters, career plans, children, owning a home, where we live, family holidays, vacation travel, the pursuit of hobbies, retirement, and much more.

There is no other person in our lives that will be more understanding of and more committed to making our goals a reality than our spouse. It is both a fun thing and a vital thing to discuss our goals together and to plan together. Then we can put our plans into action as a team and then enjoy the progress we make. Of course when obstacles block our path we work together to address those too.

This whole process brings us even closer together and unites us in the pursuit of what's important.

Over time our goals are likely to merge, to become a single set. This is part of our journey together. Very much individuals before marriage, we become one with a singularity of purpose as we travel the journey together after taking our marriage vows.

Avoid pursuing very different sets of goals at all costs. This will divide you, it will pull you apart. A few differences are fine, fundamentally different is a big deal.

Thinking practically, being divided is also likely to reduce our chances of achieving our goals. Just plain bad.

If you and your spouse have a big disagreement on one or more of your life goals, then this is a time to think and reflect and discuss. It might take some time and that is ok. Big decisions should not be rushed. Important decisions need to be considered carefully, and that takes time.

In most cases, you will find some common ground and agree to some version of the goal that both of you can support. If you are going through this process it helps to put yourself in the shoes of your spouse. Really think about this and try to understand where they are coming from and why they might have concerns. This is a healthy process.

Another important question to ask, perhaps the most important question is this—does the goal that I have make our marriage stronger? Does it threaten or negatively impact our marriage in any way? Am I being selfish? If my spouse had a similar goal, how would I feel?

This is an important time to be selfless and humble.

By now it should be no surprise that humility and selflessness come up yet again—they are at the heart of our marriage journey and find a place again here with our life goals.

Back to our goals—pursuing life goals together brings us closer and improves our chances of both being happy and united during the journey and in reaching our goals as well. Much better to fight together, than to go at it alone. That is a long and lonely road to travel and really has no place in a marriage.

It all starts with being open and completely honest about our goals with our spouse and remember this—there are no right or wrong answers here. This is our personal vision for what we want to achieve in our lives and the chances are good that your spouse will both be very interested and very understanding.

After all, they know you better than anyone.

Then, over time and after lots of honest discussion it is likely you and your spouse will come together and find common ground on these goals. Then from that point forward you are united and supportive of one another in the pursuit of your dreams. This is a wonderful thing and part of the adventure and joy that marriage can bring.

> *Encourage your spouse to dream.*
> *Encourage your spouse to chase their dreams.*
> *You will be there by their side to make it happen.*
> *Any remarkable thing we accomplish in our lives started with a dream.*

Hope

TRUTH #25

*H*ope is a wonderful thing.

A remarkable enabler of good. Hope and faith are very similar and only separated by small degrees of definition language and here we refer to faith as a fundamental belief that shapes our actions and thoughts every day. Both hope and faith look to the future and a higher good.

Because the spousal relationship is unlike any other we have with the people of our lives, marriage can be part of the higher and greater good. Hope helps to carry us there.

We marry in the hope that we will build a better life together than the life we could ever have on our own. We marry with the hope that we can and will be a better person for our spouse than the person we could ever be for ourselves. We marry in the hope that we will live our vows every day, that we will keep the sacred promises that are only made in marriage.

Hope is powerful on it's own, held by a single person, but becomes remarkably more powerful when shared in a marriage. Hope fundamentally brings more joy to every day because we carry the belief that the future holds great things for us, that the journey of life is fundamentally exciting, that the best is yet ahead.

Hope and faith make us believe that anything is possible. If we can dream it, it can happen. For our marriage, our hope calls us to believe that together we are better. Together, we can make each other the best version of our ourselves.

Hope gives us energy, hope brings us conviction, hope fuels our determination to meet and overcome challenges. Hope makes the darkest days a little brighter, and the very best days even better. There are no limits to hope shared in a marriage. This version of hope is so much bigger than what we carried when we were single.

The hope that blossoms in a marriage bears no resemblance to any version of hope when we were single. Made infinitely more powerful by the miracle of our vows.

Marriage is uniquely capable of discovering and unlocking the boundless good that hope can bring us. When we carry hope in our hearts, hold onto it and celebrate it, embrace it, magnify it, our marriage will transform in ways we could never imagine.

Hope is contagious.

If we keep hope alive while our spouse is discouraged, they are likely to come back to hope soon. Likewise, our spouse can lift us up when challenges seem overwhelming.

Everything looks different, everything looks better when we have hope and faith.

In a happy marriage, each spouse will say that the other has taught them things and shown them things they could never imagine. And, likely things they would never know without their spouse being able to open our eyes to these remarkable gifts.

A loving marriage is such a powerful source of hope because we are capable of making our hope into reality, of fulfilling the hope our spouse carries and them for us. We know them so well, we will be always on the look-out for the opportunity to make hope stronger, to reward hope for our spouse.

Hope can brings us calm, serenity in the face of the noise and clamor that surrounds us every day.

Saint Thomas Aquinas, one of history's greatest scholars and philosophers said 'To one that has faith, no explanation is necessary. To one without faith, no explanation is possible.'

Even better than making hope into reality, in our marriage we can begin to dream of what we are capable of together and this then nurtures a higher level of hope. Then with a growing sense of hope, anything is possible and our dreams are within reach.

Dreams that are impossible when we are single, become possible in our marriage. There is a big difference between playing alone and fighting the battles of life alone, *versus playing on the most powerful team on earth—the team of two created by marriage.*

When pieces of the hope we carry every day come to fruition, it makes our hope even stronger—elevates our hope to new levels not seen or not thought possible before.

Hope fuels greater and more ambitious hope.

It is often there waiting to be nurtured, we only need a little focus and encouragement to have hope carry us forward.

This is a cycle of renewal—we have dreamed new dreams and these dreams gave us hope and together we have made what we hoped for into reality, and having experienced this reality we are then naturally brought back to new dreams and the cycle starts anew.

These new dreams are then fully aware of the remarkable things that are possible in our marriage, and so our dreams become richer, fuller, more thoughtfully limitless. Our shared confidence grows, and boundaries we considered before fade away.

What this brings to us is a very simple thought, one that together we can do anything.

No challenge can stop us because together we can face it. No matter what happens, we won't be alone and this is a tremendous comfort to all of us. Everything looks different when we have our husband or wife by our side. Every day is just better, every day is fuller and more complete.

Never underestimate the connections between our twenty-five truths.

Final Thoughts

We finish where we began—with the reminder that your marriage is the single most important thing you will do in your lifetime. If you succeed at one thing, it can only be this.

Nothing else comes close.

Work, family and hobbies are important and will always be a part of our lives. But, they can't begin to match the scope and remarkable force of good that is born and grows within our marriage.

Although we have discussed twenty-five things that contribute to a happy, healthy and lasting marriage, I will close with three that stand above the others.

These three primary elements of marriage are
Love, Faith and Humility.

These powerful pillars of marriage are anything but stand-alone— they are very much intertwined with the miraculous tapestry that creates a lasting marriage.

These connections are inescapable and wonderful, the lifeblood of marriage.

We close with a simple reminder that our spouse is one of a kind, a living miracle. Together, we can become a source of unimaginable good that can only be created through the union that is marriage.

If we give our unconditional and selfless love to our spouse from the very beginning or through an awakening sometime later, this is far more important than the content and quality of our actions because over time, the greatness of our love will conquer everything else. All that we think, all that we say, and all that we do will be shaped by this love.

The bad stuff that comes at us through the course of time is no match for the good of our love and our marriage.

I hope this small book has offered a few ideas that can help with the continued discovery of the little miracles held in your marriage and the daily renewal of our vows.

Try to slow life down and appreciate now, appreciate today with your spouse. There are a thousand little gifts that our marriage and our spouse brings us every day. Try to enjoy every single one. If you are waiting to make a change in your life, holding off on saying something, or delaying doing something for your spouse, don't.

Now is the time, today is the day.

Good luck and godspeed.

Kevin

www.ingramcontent.com/pod-product-compliance
Lightning Source LLC
Chambersburg PA
CBHW020355100426
42812CB00001B/73

* 9 7 8 0 5 7 8 2 1 0 0 9 4 *